Sleeping Among Yaks

Sleeping Among Yaks

DAVID HEALEY

THE CHOIR PRESS

Copyright © 2018 David Healey

All rights reserved. No part of this publication may be reproduced or transmitted in any form or by any means, electronic or mechanical including photocopying, recording or any information storage or retrieval system, without prior permission in writing from the publishers.

The right of David Healey to be identified as the author of this work has been asserted by him in accordance with the Copyright, Designs and Patents Act 1988

First published in the United Kingdom in 2018 by
The Choir Press

ISBN 978-1-911589-53-2

Acknowledgements

I would like to thank Nicola Healey for her very helpful constructive criticism, Bob Curtis for our monthly sharing of poems, Michael Laskey and the Suffolk Poetry Group for their scrutiny and Felixstowe Café Poets for being such a good audience.

Without my wife, Ann, many of these poems would not have recovered from their childhood illnesses or been fed and watered.

Heartfelt thanks to Archie, Lyndy and Nathan Jennings for involving me in Archie's life. Archie was born on 4th of May 2010 with brain damage and is the subject of eleven poems in this collection.

I'm lucky to have had the support and encouragement of my family, whom I sometimes neglected to write these poems, in particular my daughter, Charlotte, and son, Theo.

'A Wild Swan Feed at Welney' was awarded first prize in The Crabbe Poetry Competition, 2014; 'The Canoeist', second prize in 2011; and 'An Approximation to Knowing You' was highly commended in 2017. 'Opening the Lock' won the My Stour Valley poetry competition in 2013. 'Excavation at Must Farm Quarry' was shortlisted for the Plough Poetry Prize in 2016.

'New Arrival', 'Otter' and 'Landguard Point' were previously published by *Smiths Knoll*. 'Awakening' was the title poem of an anthology celebrating the first year of the Felixstowe Café Poets.

Contents

Acknowledgements	v
SOUTH WEST	1
Otter	2
Landlake	3
The Fishermen	4
For Michael	5
Launceston Castle	6
Digging Deep	7
Taking Mum out to Lunch	8
The Townsman	10
Revival at Minack Open Air Theatre	12
The Crossing	13
Bant's Carn Burial Site, Scilly	14
Charting a Position	15
Selecting Postcards of Old Shipwrecks at Mumford's Newsagents, Scilly	16
The Ship Figurehead Museum, Tresco	17
Porth Hellick	18
FELIXSTOWE	19
Landguard Point	20
The Canoeist	21
Beach Hut Parade	22
The Radar Girl	
R.A.F Bawdsey	23
Taking a Break	24
Broad I.F.F	25
How I Join the Military	26
Snow Buntings at Christmas	27
Test Results	28
The Dory	29
The Flood	30

ARCHIE 31

New Arrival 32
The Result 33
A Mother's Song 34
Awakening 35
The Mountaineer 36
The Sensory Room 37
First Day at the Centre 38
A Wild Swan Feed at Welney 39
An Approximation to Knowing You 40
Limbs 41
Resurrection 42

OUT AND ABOUT 43

Opening the Lock 44
The Innkeeper's Wife 45
Pencil Work 46
Covehithe 47
Excavation at Must Farm Quarry 48
Dreamings 49
Antony Gormley's Another Place 50
Ourselves Wherever We are Found in Art 51
Missing You at Moissac 52
Check-in 53
The Interior 54
A Low Blood Count at Iqualuit 55
Swimming with Plankton 56
The Excursion 57
Shingle 58
South of San Francisco 59
The Tsunami Evacuation Road 60
Pelicans at Half Moon Bay 61

Notes 63

SOUTH WEST

'See where the stream-path is!
Crossing is not as hard as you might think.'

— 'Eden Rock', Charles Causley

Otter

Imagine it lying on the bank,
how disappointed you'd be
at its museum posture, its crass way of chewing fish.

Instead, you have a sighting of faster river colour,
a feeling of it being here,
ease beyond that of water, a neat disappearance.

The roughness of its coat during a scratch,
whiskers, a glassy-looking eye, perhaps its snout:
none of these you actually see

but you're left with the doubt required for belief,
the otter forever swimming
through your memory of this river crossing,

Trekelland Bridge over The Inny,
faster shallows, a deeper stillness and a glimpse
from its parapet, but enough.

Landlake

Only a brook runs through the valley
and the slate and granite bridge
is just wide enough
for a narrow van to cross.

Like Piper's Pool
with no obvious pool
and nothing for sale at Congdon's Shop,
there's no lake at Landlake.

As for the weather
you may as well ask a cow
facing you round the corner of a lane
for the forecast.

Some memories are dressed in myth
and therefore distorted.
Others wait to be repeated
but never can be.

We can't drop sticks
into the fastest current
to win a race anymore
or make a dam we'd then destroy.

On my last visit
the brook was in spate,
water tied round pillars of the bridge.
One day, perhaps a lake.

The Fishermen

Three brothers in a boat and you can see
them casting their lines far out and wide,
their lives easy then as the days were free.

A dawn mist and coots call explosively
from the reeds. Lines loose over the side.
Three brothers in a boat and you can see

their floats dipping, then a tugging lightly
from below before a pulling like the tide,
their lives easy then as the days were free.

Their bucket filled and despite rivalry
they celebrate their total catch with pride.
Three brothers in a boat and you can see

on a tray three rows of perch, their trophy,
fish shining bright, fresh and clear-eyed,
their lives easy then as the days were free.

But the years did what years do, slowly
innocent joy was lost, but what never died
were those three brothers fishing happily,
their lives easy then as the days were free.

For Michael

We were buddies back then.
Now we're old cronies
in touch occasionally
at Christmas or family deaths.
We used to sit upstairs
in the two and nines
rather than mix with other kids
in the cheaper stalls.

We'd emerge dazzled by sun
looking for our horses
tied up outside the saloon
or, as Richard Todd,
we'd gaze at torpedoed
German battleships going
down, with a theme tune
lodged in our heads.

Scared what townsfolk
would say to our dads,
of letting the side down,
we played cricket at home
rather than loiter in the street
wearing jeans and speaking
like they do in *West Side Story*
or *The Arms* in *Lanson*.

D.H. Lawrence novels
did it for us, and watching
convent school girls
from behind a laurel hedge.
It kept us safe from riding
motor bikes, wasting hours
swearing repeatedly to impress,
fitting in with nasty gangs.

Launceston Castle

Steps straight up then they curve
inside thick walls to the windy top,
sunbeams and a slanting shower.

Below are slate walls and roofs,
towers and spires, pinnacles, eaves
and the turret of The Liberal Club.

In the distance: England, an ever-
present threat of further takeovers
from the other side of the Tamar.

Launceston, already overrun
by a cash and carry then Tesco
offering better deals out of town.

The sheep and cattle markets
are now pay and displays. Across
the A30 is a new health centre.

In the square, taxis muster in ranks.
Only the castle and its battlements
resist surrendering to change.

We're told we must move on,
but I stay awhile to feel obsolete,
to save the original of who I am.

Digging Deep

She has one of those tablet things
that tell you just about everything
you do or don't need to know.
Puts me in my place, I can tell you.

After two days at The Hollies
she's already badgered the chapel
for their records, scanned the church
register for Healeys and Cooks

and ordered me a Samsung Galaxy
S6 online, telling me to email her
should I have a problem. *You can't
live without a smartphone, Uncle.*

She'll be off soon to find herself
somewhere else. There's nothing
in our village to keep her here,
nothing but a chippy, Spar and pub.

An hour ago, she uncovered a great
grandfather on the passenger list
of the S.S. Albion to Australia.
Not a convict, mind, but a miner.

Descendants are cropping up
down under as we speak. Wouldn't
put it past her to find Kylie Minogue
or Shane Warne among our lot.

Taking Mum out to Lunch

*It's always such a palaver
going out*, she used to say
before her stroke, checking
if we've checked on things,
putting the alarm on, then
finding we've left a wallet,
umbrella or gloves behind.

This morning, care assistants
give her a bath before
they put her in something nice
while we wait downstairs
with our second cup of coffee,
Dad and I talking in earnest
about the news and sport.

It's fifteen minutes in the car:
Mum hunched in the front
while I hold her shoulders
should she fall sideways.
Then it's action stations
getting the ambulance chair
out of the boot, strapping her in

taking her where potholes,
tractor ruts, aisles and gaps
require sharp turns and twists.
We aim towards a farm shop;
once inside, we zigzag past
fruit and veg, dried flowers,
chutneys, mustards and pies.

In the café, she feeds herself
mince, though we're on hand
with tissues if she misses,
should she spill gravy down
her chin. She's holding on
for longer. We're holding on,
doing alright by her, we think.

The Townsman

i.m. Arthur Bate Venning, 1919–2017

He was in front of his house opposite
at some stage during our visits home.
Warmth flowed from him
like a break in the clouds,
his Cornish accent straight
as a pass from scrum to fly half
across Dunheved Road.
A supporter on the touch line
whenever my brothers played
for Launceston Rugby Football Club.

He'd ask how Mum and Dad were
whenever they were ill
with the tact of a man who valued the privacy
of his neighbours and what they did.
Mum worked like him
for The Eventide Trust
supporting the sick, elderly and frail
and Dad, he'd call *Doctor*,
bestowing on him the status
he believed was due.

Broad-shouldered yet gentle,
he looked out for people
while preserving the memory of those
who had gone: 'If you don't write it down
your memories will be lost.'
Author of *The Book of Launceston*,
retired editor of *The Cornwall
and Devon Post*, he was around to listen
before there were mobile phones
and social media.

Only recently did I read he served
in the Army for six years during the war.
Bard of the Cornish Gorsedh,
burgess of the town,
Dad would keep us posted about Arthur
across the road, his loyalty
to Launceston where we used to live
never feeling we belonged
anywhere else since we left.
It's why we needed him back home.

Revival at Minack Open Air Theatre

Twice, we lose our way driving here,
the mist so dense we mistake a standing
stone for a telephone kiosk, and cairns
for cows. We skip the café and shop,
the recorded intro into Rowena Cade's
creation of the theatre out of a cliff face
and make for the gods. There's no
Shakespeare or Gilbert and Sullivan
today, just a couple on separate podiums
filming each other with their iPhones.
The agaves and aeoniums behind us
are clumsy and oversized alongside
native rock samphire, thyme and thrift.
Everything's displaced; even our dead
parents require us to imagine them alive,
never getting older. Past visits here
end up being rehearsals for futures
we were never cast in. Then light clips
the granite seating and opens the view
between Carracks and Logan Rock,
so much blue revealed and gannets
circling higher on the thermals before
they drop, wings not quite folded back,
closing just as they finish their dive.

The Crossing

A late start. The Scillonian turns into Mount's Bay.
So far so good. Off Mousehole, though, we feel
the first surge downwards and back up,
the roll alternates sky with sea
through every porthole.

Why we didn't stay behind for a day, and visit
Lanyon Quoit and the Merry Maidens
followed by a lobster supper at Marazion,
I'll never know.

Past Longships, the Irish sea adds further swell.
Several on deck are vomiting into paper bags.
We focus on the horizon, tell each other
we're half way across and it's not long
to go now.

There's folk in Suffolk don't even know
the Isles of Scilly exist, which is hardly surprising
considering weather forecasters stand
in front of them on the map.

Sometimes I think it's just my imagination
created the islands, my own Atlantis.
With the sea ahead uncompromisingly persistent,
how can shores arise from all this turmoil
and offer such peace?

Bant's Carn Burial Site, Scilly

We were picnicking on its outer ledge;
Dad, being Mum, careful not to spill
any juice or make a sticky mess.

The only place I saw him eat an orange,
slowly peeled with his penknife,
the skin becoming one complete helix.

I imagined Bronze Age man
preparing his next meal: flensing
a seal with a new metal blade.

Half a century later I'm remembering
when we crouched inside
to keep us dry during a downpour.

Flood water fell over the entrance.
We plugged gaps between the capstones
with moss and turf to stop any leaks

until the sun came out and we emerged
with all the islands laid out before us,
his gift to me ever since.

Charting a Position

We saw South Star at Mousehole quay
a week or two back when he'd told us
it was a Scottish trawler he'd renovated
these last few years.

Vegetables were growing on the foredeck.
There were solar panels on the cabin roof.
His partner was hanging washing on a line
stretching fore to aft.

He talked then as if we were mates
not nosey tourists. Now, he waves at us
from his boat at Porth Seal, Scilly.
All I know about him

is that he chucked his job in the city
to live as he does and not harm the planet,
a steady course of conviction
with good anchorage.

Selecting Postcards of Old Shipwrecks at Mumford's Newsagents, Scilly

It was three miles south-east of Land's End
when it struck a rock, like something bad happening
in a marriage. Sails furled. Looks good,
but the Yankee windjammer is holed,
its cargo of wheat swelling, the timbers soon to part.
The ship could be a model in this sooty photograph
and the lady, peering through a telescope, staged
on her curve of cliff. The crew took to the boats
and were saved, while we are shamed
by wanting more visible evidence of distress.

Only one cow is left of the 400 or so head of cattle
saved at up to £5 each for salvage. It stands
against the background of a herd of rocks
such that you might miss seeing it at first.
The Castleford is one side of the frame
and, just visible, Bishop Rock light on the other.
The fog has cleared and the sea is calm
as it needed to be for the photographer
to get there safely. Islanders have come and gone,
already claiming they were first to the wreck.

The picnic appears planned on granite boulders
beside a holiday sea, everyone contemplating
their enjoyment. But it's only men sitting there,
no children dipping their nets into a pool.
Behind them, at 20 degrees, a metal hull
complains where it is, too huge to be hauled
by any winch. A dark room joke, perhaps,
one plate over another, some allegory or time warp,
until we read they boarded again at the next tide
and sailed away, never taking their caps off.

The Ship Figurehead Museum, Tresco

Some have a name, some not.
Lady Falkland resides not far
from a painted shepherdess.
Friar Tuck was powerless to stop
his namesake, a tea-clipper,
from breaking up in a gale,
nor could a Spanish lady prevent
her laden barque from striking
The Crims with a cargo of guano
and hooves from Valparaiso.

Perhaps they salvage pride
being in mess kit or smart dress,
proud-bosomed or sash-breasted,
looming over us with restored
authority. In T-shirts and shorts
we drift aimlessly about,
discovering when and how
they arrived here, what salvage
or shock discovery on a beach
one day enabled their refit.

Porth Hellick

You're quick to spot the shapes
of a Loaded Camel and Shrimp
in the outline of granite boulders
and find Sir Cloudesley Shovell's
monument, commemorating
himself and his ghastly mistake:
four warships sunk in one night
with a loss of two thousand men.

Below us the *SS Lady Charlotte*
was wrecked in 1917. Across
the porth the Cita ran aground
twenty years ago on the point
after the night watch fell asleep.
There are no bodies floating in
on the tide, though a porpoise,
surfacing, shocks us a bit.

There's no broken spar or mast,
though we mistake a dark shadow
on the sea for a spreading slick
and find more recent wreckage
in the strandline: torn seine net
wrapped round a dead puffin,
degreasing canisters, Bic biros
and half a plastic purple giraffe.

FELIXSTOWE

So many moods of light, sky,
Such a flux of cloud shapes,
Cloud colours blending, blurring,
And the winds, to be learnt by heart:
So much movement to make a staying.

— 'In Suffolk', Michael Hamburger

Landguard Point

Even if the universe is leaking protons or whatever,
though it's difficult to imagine where to exactly,
or the sun is running out of its fuel supply,
I'm not going to sweat over it, not now, not here

where the shoreline waits for a watercolourist
and a fully-loaded container ship slips silently by
above the sea kale. The rabbits aren't fazed,
they continue feeding wherever there's grass.

A dragonfly hawks the tamarisk. A breeze picks up
and light catches the outline of a ruined jetty.
These observable events might belong to gravity
but also to what the dead may be dreaming about.

Everything has its strategy to be noticed.
The morning exhibits concrete. The boarded-up café
has, so far, resisted being broken into, and clouds
are reflected in the black glass of H.M. Customs.

Fourteen billion light years from Earth, galaxies
are moving away, deep space is littered with them.
Meanwhile, a man with his dog says good morning
and wheatears perch on the torn perimeter fence.

The Canoeist

This morning, I see him through my telescope
eating his lunch, taking a nap or just sitting
buoyant as a gull in the air against the wind,
not bothered by any swell, it would seem.
After finishing my shopping, he's still there
as if to avoid being cooped up in Morrisons,
a traffic jam or office, should disaster strike.

Better to be behind a tsunami than face it,
to slalom round martello and church towers
than drown inside an Audi or B.M.W.
When the North Sea breaches our defences
he'll be first to rescue those trapped upstairs,
pets and grannies, to deliver babies and help
those marooned on higher ground to survive.

He'll have matches and a Swiss Army knife.
Who can say? A century or more from now,
worshippers might stretch back to the A12
from the islands of Felixstowe and Trimley
just to touch the hem of his canoe, to feel
his frail ark, to be given strength to paddle,
correct a capsize and meet deadlines of tide.

Beach Hut Parade

There could be all sorts happening
at *Her Place* and *Gulls and Buoys,*
rumours starting in *Vicar's Rest*
and goings on in *Mother's Ruin.*
But at Jean's hut the padlocked bar
stays across. She's been absent
all summer. Avril says she's left
Arthur, and can't afford the rent.

There's a crossword to finish at *Us*
and racing results at *Happy Days,*
but the future has already happened
at *Dogger Bank*: granny's swiping
her smartphone; she's on Facebook.
Wind turbines wind up the sea
and loaded container ships queue
to enter the docks at Felixstowe.

Those in deck chairs at *'ere we be*
sunbathe as in a Hopper painting,
pensioners breathing the sea air
ignorant of levels of toxic emissions.
Who knows where the kids have gone,
who the piper is at *The Lookout.*
Someone will be waiting for results.
Someone will arrive with the news.

The Radar Girl

R.A.F Bawdsey

Six-hour spells in the Operations Room
measuring range, direction and elevation

needed good eyes, quick brains and stamina.
Not surprising they chose women for the work

though one green male flight lieutenant
needed convincing we weren't put on this earth

to stay at home and have kids. Not all of us
were posh graduates. June was an office girl.

Ann's father owned the garage at Trimley.
She knew a thing or two about engineering.

We had to be ready for any raid. There was
no switching off or taking a cigarette break.

We were billeted in rat-infested attic rooms
at the manor. The men were in wooden huts

but it didn't stop us imitating Lady Muck
descending the grand staircase for dinner.

No ironed linen table cloths though, or being
waited upon like the WRENS at Harwich.

Taking a Break

The lily pond and topiary were a world away
from consoles, receivers and transmitters.

After hours of plotting aircraft positions
some of us would go there to unwind;

others, on hot days, relaxed in civvies
on the cordoned-off, mine-free section of beach.

If I wanted to escape gossip about boyfriends
I'd look for Charlie, somewhere in the woods.

Wounded at Ypres, the Quilters let him
have a tithe cottage for the rest of his days.

I'd watch him repair the extensive fence
that kept foxes out, not with chicken wire

but much stronger army stuff he'd managed
to get hold of. Charlie's Suffolk brogue

was so gentle, it didn't matter if I failed
to understand what he was saying. I learnt

just by being with him, helping to put
dead leaves in the basket for composting,

sharing his silence as if it was a bunker
safe from any attack of pain, fear or loss.

Broad I.F.F.

Last May, a Dornier 217K
was shot down directly over Bawdsey
just missing the school,
and once or twice Focke Wulf 190s
flew low and strafed the village.

I couldn't tell you this at the time, Mummy,
even if I'd wanted to,
because I knew you'd get in a tizz.
Besides, our work was top secret
and our letters censored.

Doodlebugs were worse.
If the sound of their engines
cut out overhead, it was curtains.
One of them exploded close to the lightship,
another on the beach.

It's not easy since Ivor went missing,
seeing others having a jolly time.
I'm left with blips
of thirty 'Lancs' going out,
knowing he was flying one of them

and not being able to say to him
I love you so much.
I have flashbacks to our bombers
showing SOS (broad I.F.F.)
and think it's him trying to get home.

I remember Stanmore coordination HQ
asking us to follow them closely,
in particular, which we did,
then getting a visual on them chugging in
painfully slow, losing height.

How I Join the Military

It's not easy convincing blokes half pissed
they're disturbing a pair of Little Terns
nesting feet away from their beach barbecue.
Nor does suggesting they'll get more peace
if they move elsewhere cut much ice
when the revellers haven't even noticed
the frantic alarm calls and swooping dives
just above their shaved and sunburnt heads.

Knowing the enemy is key. Pot bellies
don't shout members of the armed forces
who've just returned from Afghanistan.
Mentioning that an explosive device
was reported where they've set up base
may fool them sufficiently. But, saying
I'm sent ahead to warn folk, that may need
props, a piece of metal looking like a mine.

This brings me to an old satellite dish
acquired courtesy of Sky, small enough
for my backpack, large enough to look
explosive if stepped on. Secretly, I'd bury
the device so it's visible in the shingle
and slip into my army surplus uniform
as they splash each other in the sea or throw
a Frisbee about as their charcoal heats up.

Then, it's just a matter of presenting myself
with bomb-disposal confidence. I'd indicate
the danger, warn them there's a timer set
to go off and ask their help to clear the area
before the rest of my crew arrive. Meanwhile
their slabs of meat would wait to be cooked.
The Little Terns' eggs are cooling. Minutes
are ticking away. Any moment a loss of life.

Snow Buntings at Christmas

There's been all sorts of erosion this year:
coastal, loved ones dying, a further reduction
in the numbers of most of our native species.
But here, at least, is a celebration. Light catches
the white outer tail feathers and wing patches
of snow buntings as they take off and fly over
our heads with a rippling *tirrirrip tirrirrip*
set against the sibilant retreat of sea on shingle.

Nineteen is an easy number to count in flight,
but on the ground they frequently disappear
in a dip, or behind last summer's sea kale leaves.
So, if you come this way and don't know
they are here, you may think Landguard Point
is empty of life, that no birth happens, no star
shines brighter than others and no kings
bearing gifts would travel such a distance.

Test Results

His van's parked tight up against a hedge.
He's digging for *lugs* most likely.
I could say nothing, put the rogue cells
invading his body out of my mind,
the anaemia, infections and bleeding
he's likely to get, and instead
watch him out on the mud, his shadow
extending much further than himself
as if he's the gnomon of a sun dial
whose time I could easily turn back.

He'll need chemo, radiotherapy and blood,
maybe a marrow transplant.
Better to get on with it. He'll not like
the lines connecting him up as if he's
some sort of bait, being penned
into a cubicle and told to stay put.
Though he never kept a woman for long,
plenty will fuss around him soon,
call him Alec, though they've only just met,
tell him what he can and can't do.

Sky reddens from the west. His bucket's
full. Soon he'll come this way
and comment to the effect *I'll not catch
many fish with a stethoscope.*
He'll know something's not right
about his tests, but not ask directly.
I'm thinking how best to start, whether
there's any way to cushion the facts
when they fall on him and how to care
without my job getting in the way.

The Dory

What's confusing is what's
been used in the past.
See this! It's the wrong stuff
after the boat was rammed into;
this is polystyrene
needing a different paint
to the bottom that's fibreglass.

It'll take a while to prepare.
Not been looked after
for years, I shouldn't wonder.
Then, there's the primer,
several coats, top
and anti-fouling to put on,
gout and weather permitting.

Should look good as new
when I've finished.
Perhaps you know of medicine
that'll do the same, doc,
though you'll get no rest
when they find out
you've a cure for old age.

And rest is what both of us
need more of, I reckon,
less repairing. You, hanging up
your stethoscope,
though I'm sure you'll
still use it occasionally,
and me, doing lighter jobs.

The Flood

*Better to keep an old tractor we know how to repair than buy
a modern sort with newfangled options and electrics that go wrong.
Besides, searching online for a new component can take all day;
even then you have to wait for cows to die before receiving it.*

He took off his shirt. The dressing underneath was soiled.
*Can't keep the dirt away, not when the river's flooding. They lost
their pigs at Meadow Farm and Ed Faircroft hasn't had much luck
with his hens either; he'll have nothing left besides some insurance*

*that's if he gets it. Water needs good run off, plenty of space to rise
and drains deeper than councils decide. Floods teach this without
any need for computers or exams. Water doesn't wait for paperwork
to be completed or what assessors at Norwich Union throw at us.*

I could see the wound was worse, the rolled edges more emphasised.
He knew. Joked about his time soon being up. I gave him my usual
more positive forecast, hedging my bets he'd be around long enough
to see a better summer than this one, but didn't look him in the eye.

ARCHIE

Grey waters, vast
 as an area of prayer
that one enters. Daily
 over a period of years
I have let the eye rest on them.
Was I waiting for something?

— 'Sea-watching', R.S. Thomas

New Arrival

I'd need to shift my position
among the other visitors
to see the length of him
immaculately wrapped.
So much hushed joy. Flowers
not allowed since my day.
Nowhere to put the card
except on the bedside locker
and that's already crowded.

I can see his head end on,
the fontanelles I used
to feel for in the birth canal.
I'm subsidiary, retired,
one of his granddads,
but want to be more:
his guru and coach
in the karate kid films,
his regular goalkeeper.

I've lost the breezy
white-coated certainty
that let me through before
ID necklaces and digital keys.
Instead, I wait at the back.
Someone else has counted
his fingers, examined
his hips and base of spine
and written in his notes.

The Result

It begins okay with reassuring stuff
about his head circumference and weight,
but the second paragraph
is quickly into abnormalities
on CT scan: *leuco* something *acia*
associated with prenatal insult,
cause unknown.

It's why his development's delayed,
the letter says, and why
he's not talking yet or standing up.
On the floor, all this time,
Archie continues what he can do
using his weak hand to hold
what he fails to explore.

The family wanting to learn
what the future holds
also prefer not to know
or believe what the specialist has written.
Avoiding eye contact,
we gaze down and watch Archie
prise apart his galaxy of toys.

A Mother's Song

We muddle through, you and I.
At three years old you clap
then check to see I'm doing the same.
You can't walk unsupported
though you tiptoe
when certain muscles tighten
when they shouldn't.

Nothing's complete or guaranteed.
We celebrate the incidental
flickering of light
on the ceiling
or a breeze of bubbles,
your smile quick as a shoal of fish
or flock on the turn.

Sometimes, when I look at your eyes,
you're in a wonderland
only you have a visa for
because everyone else
is thinking too much,
living with regret
or scared of the future.

The universe with its black holes
and nebulae doesn't concern us
and never shall.
What matters are the ducks
waddling towards us, and bird song
that used to frighten you
but doesn't any more.

Awakening

Each day
the water level
rises up the buddhas.
They're not bothered,
don't flinch or resort to
higher ground to sit with
the reclining sculpture
at Wat Pho temple
in Bangkok
or do anything besides
going under, letting their studded hair,
topped with a spike, stick above the flood.
We'll never know, Archie, how your brain
got swamped inside your mother's womb
nor why the joy in your eyes belongs
to a breeze through foliage or sunlight
revealing the mountain tops at last.
You are sleeping among yaks in Tibet
keeping yourself warm and safe despite rising
fuel costs and turmoil in the world's financial markets.
You inhabit time and space like a flock of alpine choughs
and will never attend a conference on the Higgs boson particle
or find an avalanche of obstacles on your path to enlightenment.

The Mountaineer

He knows, just by crawling across
the hall to the foot of the stairs
that I'll help him climb them.
It's the first thing he wants to do
recently, when he's visiting us,
because the bungalow he lives in
only has hills, not proper mountains.

I wonder if he's pleased to see me
and if I count in his team of stars
and clouds. I often watch his face
for any sign I belong to his ranges,
to the colossal spaces he roams
above the tree line, where ice
is steep and crampons are needed.

Sometimes, he looks behind him
to check I'm there. He's giving me
more slack to play with. The rope
holds us both as he takes on more
stairs. I daren't tell his mum
how dizzy I get coming down.
At the bottom he climbs again.

The Sensory Room

Colours flow upwards
inside lava lamps,
your own northern lights.
Bubbles don't pop.
We're here to calm you down,
though it's me
who softens into sleep,
catching myself snoring
looking after you.
Soothed too much by a slow
singing of *wheels on the bus*
and the magic carpet, so bouncy,
any minute I may levitate.

Waves, projected on a screen,
aren't like any we've seen
from the beach at Felixstowe,
but I whisper *Look Archie!*
Mr Sea. Whoosh whoosh
and you eagerly point
to your other palm,
Makaton sign language
for wanting more,
whether it's the waves,
repeating my *whooshing*
or you picking up on us
sharing something.

First Day at the Centre

I don't know where to look
or put my hands;
the children, they need
so much help.
Jake asks if I'd like a coffee.
He's a nightclub bouncer.
His partner's a beautician.
They do different shifts.

It's craft next, we're told,
then sensory corner.
There are mats and mirrors,
lava lamps, wobbly dolls
that never fall over
and mothers in the yoga position
supporting their children
from behind.

Thomas, Jake's four year old,
still can't read or talk.
He's praised by the staff
for his finger painting
while Lyndy, Archie's mum,
is chatting to Lucy's mum, Jane,
about the leg splints
they have to use.

We do favourite songs
and Luke's Happy Birthday.
Lyndy beckons me to the floor
beside my grandson, Archie.
We make waterfalls
and play at rainbows.
I blow bubbles between
my finger and thumb.

A Wild Swan Feed at Welney

After the kerfuffle of reaching
the viewing chamber, making sure
the children with additional needs
don't get lost or left behind

the swans fly towards us,
strung out like a wavering horizon,
glide down and carve Vs of curved
spray as they water ski to a stop.

The children laugh and cry, call
across to each other, answer back.
As soon as grain is thrown
from a barrow, the swans converge

snatch and swallow what they can,
near enough for us to see
each adult bird has a wedge
of yellow on its bill.

There's bugling and honking
on the lagoon. Most are Whoopers,
though the warden in his spiel
informs us Bewick swans

are seen better from East Hide.
It's a rumpus when they take off:
smack smack against water
as they struggle to get airborne.

Archie, my grandson, can't stand
without splints and hand rails,
but flapping his arms like wings,
he gives me the lift I need just now.

Pools of sunlight and cloud shadow
sweep across The Ouse Washes.
When I hold him at the window
he laughs at where he is in the sky.

An Approximation to Knowing You

Sometimes I think you fumble
at the door of creation and aren't sure
if you're moulding the waves
or if it's me winding up the sea
as I do your toy car or music box.

A lobe is absent on your brain scan
and there's thinning of your cortex,
which is why you can't stand
and need constant supervision
should you break the flat-screen tele.

Only able to utter a few words
you use Makaton sign language
when wanting a drink, biscuit,
your tablet to play with or red bus,
signing as quick as jack springing

from his box, while I take time
with my swollen arthritic fingers
and poor memory to signify
what it is I'm trying to convey.
We laugh a lot though. We manage.

In summer, wheeling you into town,
we pass under an avenue of limes.
You look up to see the leaves
fluttering and swaying above us.
It's often what we do, you and I,

watch light tremble and escape
through foliage and form liquid
patterns on the earth below.
It's how our two minds meet
and flow beyond what limits us.

Limbs

He uses, best he can, the sparse
neural pathways left to him

to rise and remain upright,
but falls over like the day-old

foal of a Suffolk Punch, limbs
already as long as its mother's.

Six today, he shows his grandpa
what he can do without splints,

looking over his shoulder to see
I'm watching, then braces himself

by holding onto the back of a chair,
managing to stay on his legs.

Mo Farrow wins, but off the track
another victory breaks the tape

just as glorious, less newsworthy,
but worth a medal nonetheless.

Resurrection

We kneel in silent prayer
but suddenly Archie shouts.
Some in the congregation
are annoyed, others smile.

All is not lost this Easter
for we go outside to visit
the man nailed to a cross
with roof above his head,

his hands just low enough
for Archie to reach and feel
moss growing in his palms,
the fingers half flexed.

I wonder if he's waiting
for Christ to spring to life
like frogs on his tablet,
provided it's charged.

Does he see the stone cross
as the splints he had to wear
after his recent hip op,
the man asleep for now?

Archie will have none of it!
He rises from his wheelchair
and, fast as a thief, pulls
at Christ's beard and hair.

OUT AND ABOUT

Oh, must we dream our dreams
and have them, too?
And have we room
for one more folded sunset, still quite warm?

— 'Questions of Travel', Elizabeth Bishop

Opening The Lock

He'd dawdle by the river
as often as not
to avoid working in the office,
neglected bushel counts
to sketch elms, clouds and haywains

and once drew me opening and closing
a lock gate to let a barge
into another level;
said he'd put me in a painting
not as Adonis but myself

as he did Ned
shaving a strake to fit a hull
in 'Boat-Building near Flatford Mill'.
Who would have thought
we'd ever grace a gallery or drawing room,

that, reduced in size,
we'd matter as much as a spire
rising above the tree tops
or nobility painted larger than life
in all their finery

and that Lucy's boy
would remain forever the same age
by drinking from a pool
on the way to a cornfield
in a summer that never lost its leaves.

The Innkeeper's Wife

Until that night
I felt I didn't matter much.
We weren't getting on, my husband and I.

Guests complained.
The girls were fractious
and often late to work.

I woke to cries from the stable
and crossed the yard to have a look.
The goat was on guard, bless him.

A man mopped his wife's brow.
A bright star shone through the roof
we still hadn't mended.

Birth looked imminent
so I knelt down, telling her
when to push and not to push

easing the baby's head out slowly.
His body followed with the waters.
He cried. I cut the cord

and handed him to her.
Never before had I felt such relief
from drudgery and darkness.

Little did I know at the time
who the baby was. It was busy.
A lot was going on.

Pencil Work

Dr Edward Wilson 1872–1912

During summer, I finish my Antarctic
landscapes outdoors, taking with me
my home-made, bad-weather sketching box.

Throughout winter, confined to the hut,
I draw, under oil lamps: tubenoses, tarsi,
hooked bill ends, eyelids and wide gapes,

evidence enough of God's own attention
to intricate detail. For smallest anatomy
I resort to mounted eye glass and chin rest,

each structure, during dark days, drawn
with a harder graphite. For differences
in snow, ice and sky, soft pencil is best.

Frozen snow, I suggest by absence
of pencil work when indicating inclines
or slight dips with shading elsewhere.

A dark line of emperor penguins greeted us
at Cape Crozier, dense and noisy life
after nothing but blizzards and crevasses.

No shade this time to depict their distant
black contrast against the tall ice shelf,
just the sharp point of a 6B for each bird.

Covehithe

He is nearer to us than we are to ourselves
St Augustine

No roof. No way down to the crypt. Steps up
to the rood loft are blocked. Most tracery
is gone from the gothic arches,
leaving only broken curls and question marks.

I'm clinging to the hope there's more
than a worn saint or grinning face of a gargoyle,
that love can be realized without
a familiar person or voice.

Nothing's overt or immediate. I know that.
There has to be patience and a letting go,
a loss before finding more. The lane ends
at a cliff edge and there's the sea

confident as a tearaway. But the distances
are too great. On the horizon
a container ship floats half sunk.
The sky's too busy altering its weather.

I need proximity to assist belief:
a moth hovering millimetres away in a rose
or the flock of curlew flying low overhead,
their calls, wild yet intimate.

Excavation at Must Farm Quarry

It happened so quickly; your wife
weaving colour into a summer cloak
and you taking a nap after hunting crane,
both huts going up in flames. Thousands
of years later, you're back, your home
now an archaeological site inside a tent.
The palisade is still in place, the burnt
rafters fallen in, your baldric ring
and sword we're easing from the ground.

Already you've decided we owe you
something for the forest we cleared
and marsh we drained: my binoculars
that conquer distance top your list
and my Mitsubishi, faster than deer,
aiming moonbeams deep into night.
We invent a sign language on the hoof,
you and I, a sort of Makaton and try
to reach an understanding as best we can.

You're alarmed by lines, stretching
high over land, held up by identical
leafless trees, the thin dark blades
we often talk into and the vast number
of buildings with so many floors.
You wonder if the spirits are angry,
if there's any going back, if you'll
ever see your wife and child again
and why the horizon burns at night.

Dreamings

You send a text from Bangkok asking if I'd clean out
Teacake's hutch, a job you'd forgotten to do
before leaving.

From Darwin, you post a card of the Thorny Devil,
often seen on bitumen roads in sand dune country,
a spiny lizard

not even you, Dad, could dream up. Two months
into your walkabout, I receive a letter
from South Alligator

*where the Rainbow Serpent gave birth to forest
and where the sun and stars came out of the ground
at the start of everything.*

Then nothing for weeks. Headline news reports
British backpackers have gone missing
in the outback.

At last, an email with pictures of you attached.
Your shadow extends across hummocks of spiniflex
at Ayres Rock.

At Tennant Creek, you pose between split halves
of a giant granite egg. A new boyfriend took the photos,
a geology student

studying land forms for his PhD. You're well into
your dreamtime now. The horizon doesn't settle.
You're a long way off.

Antony Gormley's Another Place

Criss-crossing tracks going nowhere
in particular and random casts

of the same man standing dark
in a wash of light at Crosby beach,

barnacled, especially in their creases,
tarnished, a nicer word for rust,

not to be messed with, I shouldn't wonder
but requiring acknowledgement:

one is half submerged,
another, his head only just above the tide

and all of them far enough away
from each other to be alone

until dense flocks of waders turn
this way and that together in flight

calling a repeated *kip* or shrill *peep*
or quieter *krree, poo-eep, whet whet*

under parts suddenly illuminated
then switched off again.

I'm sculpting my own presence here
as a figure in the landscape

facing distant wind turbines
and what lies beyond: another place

I can go to while staying put,
steadying myself against the weather.

Ourselves Wherever We are Found in Art

We occupy a bench dedicated to your Uncle Tom
and Aunt Ethel, who loved this place so much
they retired here, brought their sandwiches
to this spot, as we do. They sat discreetly apart,
like Henry Moore's King and Queen sculpture
at Glenkiln, never showing any physical contact.
Uncle Andy, on the other hand, painted nudes
like Lucian Freud, blemishes and all, embracing
each other in postures we imitated together.

I dreamt about your mum warning you about men
wanting only one thing and to be especially careful
of my sort, all charm and dash but gone in a flash.
We were models in a mural by Stanley Spencer
and ended up making love in the back garden
while she handed out cups of tea to various figures
from the New Testament, requesting on our behalf,
absolution for our sins. In town, we were featured
on stills in a cinema foyer of films coming soon.

One day, we took the 10.15 to Liverpool Street
to do a museum or watch a matinee, returning home
before the rush hour. It was your idea to visit
the Tate to see what all the fuss was about:
Tracey Emin's mattress on the floor, bed unmade,
condoms, underwear, full ash tray and a suitcase.
It might have been us who had risen from the mess,
hurriedly washed and dressed and were looking back
at the room one last time before catching the bus.

Missing You at Moissac

i.m. Terrence Hirst

You would have noticed the dragonfly
hawking between the cedar of Lebanon
and the pantiled walks
of the cloisters at Moissac.
No angel's wings beat as fast

and you would have welcomed its intrusion
among the sculptured capitals
visiting Daniel in the lion's den, one moment,
gate-crashing the wedding at Cana, the next.

But you favoured less clutter in holy places,
less elaborate props.
If there had been a sanctuary
to stop you on your journey
away from this world,
to detain you longer,
it would have been a neighbouring hillside
where lizards scribble themselves
over stone walls
and hoopoes swoop to a stop

where bells can be heard
without you knowing where they're ringing from.

Check-In

We might belong to Hochtief,
a German construction company
rewarding staff with four days
quad bike racing and jet skiing,
or be the Danish couple booked
for facials, seaweed body wraps
and volcanic hot stone massage.
But our passports are British
and however many times reception
taps at various keyboards,
our names aren't on the system.

We're allocated 519, eventually,
level 8, down a corridor hung
with Braque and Picasso prints,
disruptions like the crooked
put-together feel of the place.
Nothing is finished that was started.
I land on our bathroom floor
because the toilet seat isn't fixed.
Hot water comes out of the cold
and your bedside light comes away
from the wall with plaster attached.

So we repack and return
past works by Marc and Matisse
as far as Munch's Scream
at a lift stuck between floors.
We take the tiled stairs to the lobby
where a vast wing shape twists
upwards into cathedral space,
the architect long gone, if he ever
came at all. A wall television
silently shows a bomb blast.
Fish ogle us from an aquarium.

The Interior

We wanted to go there, simple as that,
travel up a vast river into the heart of Africa,
not see it on television or be told what it's like.

Before us: M25 tail-backs, a long delay
at Heathrow and a journey the other end
driving round floods and fallen trees.

We arrive at the Bridge 2 Far Luxury Hotel
only to find toilets blocked, taps leaking,
an infestation of ants and the restaurant closed.

In the Good Hope Bottle Bar, bauxite miners
are pissed and the Heavenly Funeral Parlour
offers discounts should we not come back.

Trouble starts when each guide claims
they're taking us in their motorised pirogue
which has to be solved with backhanders.

They call us Mr and Mrs Livingstone.
*I show you manatees and finfeet. Stick with me
I know special for you. Trust me, okay.*

We bale out water swirling round our feet,
while staring ahead where sky and river meet
in a haze. Crocodiles slip off the banks.

Already we feel in the heart of darkness
about to make first contact with cannibals
until the Real Africa Floating Burger Bar

comes round the next bend. Swanee River
is being played on deck. Not far behind,
boats are laden with Saga safari trippers.

A Low Blood Count at Iqaluit

Parking his skidoo anyhow, he chucks
his parka over a chair,
stuffs his takeaway wrapping
into a clinical disposal unit
and waits.

Piuk, they call him at the drilling station,
eskimo curlew now extinct.
He once heard a lone bird
calling in the direction
of nowhere.

Piuk, who built igloos in two hours
and whose summer tent
he pitched, surrounded
by flowers of purple
saxifrage,

watches television in his allocated prefab.
He doesn't carve greenstone anymore.
His latest blood picture
shows his white cells
reduced.

Looking down my microscope, I see
an aerial photograph of floes
with declining numbers
of ringed seals
hauled out.

Swimming with Plankton

The ocean outing comes with support vessel,
cocktails and barbecued crayfish. Today,

Michel demonstrates, down his microscope,
aggressive appendages of crustacean larvae.

For his PhD, he's studying siphonophores;
some measure as long as blue whales.

Swimming, I thank phytoplankton personally
for fifty percent of the oxygen I breathe.

I'm surrounded by polyps, tentacles, claws
and needles of fluorescent radiolarians.

The local fishermen are catching less each year.
Stars shine, but where is the phosphorescence

they lit with their oars, their evidence of heaven?
Jellyfish clog up propellers in the harbour;

they flourish. Otherwise, I feel I'm arriving
at a carnival as the decorations are coming down,

The Excursion

We never meant to go as far
as Teguise, just Tahiche
to see the cactus garden,
but the coach took us
to the old capital as well
to the aloe vera stalls,
rows of bling and T shirts,
to the Canarian folk dancers
we couldn't see for the crowd
gathered in the square.

A senior moment you said
as I mistook a male nurse
accompanying an old gent
wearing a red bandana
for our driver and guide.
Photographing two ferrets
as they perched on a donkey
I tripped over a kerb
landing heavily in the arms
of a lady from Solihull.

We waited for a passenger
who'd got lost, a widower
sitting in the wrong coach.
I was miles away wondering
how Cory's shearwaters
track their food in the ocean,
whether we'd be late for lunch
and if God visited all
the locked white churches
on our way back to Arrecife.

Shingle

My son's an expert at saying goodbye
without much fuss, putting down
enough roots elsewhere to last months,
but I'm left wondering was it me
telling him about my journeys abroad
that keeps him on the move all these years.

Each winter, it feels we're further apart
as I fix myself to the Suffolk coast,
its strandline plants, geese and tides.
I watch the sea erode and deposit,
putting myself in my son's shoes,
the ground shifting beneath his feet.

There's no catch up or return to the past.
Climbing shingle is like treading water
and walking down a ridge I cause pebble
landslides. Summers slip by without him
sleeping curled up on Thorpeness beach,
leaving behind his form, his warmth.

South of San Francisco

After turning off the six lane freeway
my taxi joins Cabrillo Highway South.
Less trucks doing 100.

Dust stings my eyes
due to the demolition of whole neighbourhoods
for luxury high rises.

The driver, Luke, voted for Trump,
America first and the wall to keep
illegal immigrants out.

We turn off for La Honda,
climb to Frank's house, Theo's father-in-law,
in good time for the barbecue.

Frank and his sisters are Mexican;
they sit with their ninety-year-old mother
round a redwood table.

I'm pleased Theo's happy, got a green card,
wants to settle down with Katherine
in a place of their own

but billion dollar techies put up prices
and buy land for ranches
to show off they have cattle.

Meanwhile, on the other side of the ocean,
Kim Yung Un boasts nuclear missiles
capable of reaching California.

The Tsunami Evacuation Road

It's an easy straight escape,
but the wave I felt engulf me
was quicker than any
five-litre mustang convertible.
In the dream, I saw the sea
sucked back as if it was kind
and harmless. Then
everything speeded up:

dog walkers screamed; barks
barely begun were cut off;
a roar drowned the song
of a Phoebe flycatcher.
I ended up kilometres inland,
wedged in a eucalyptus
alongside golfers
talking about their handicaps.

But today, there's no sign
of catastrophe or loss,
except my son's surf board
isn't where he keeps it.
He doesn't answer his calls.
No one knows where he is.
Shearwaters gather off shore.
They weren't there yesterday.

Pelicans at Half Moon Bay

On the shore, they're hunched
like awkward teenagers,
their bikes crashed beneath them.
They hang their wings out to dry,
gaps between pinions, heads
bent, bodies partly broken.
As wind builds in the bay
their bill pouches flap like fabric
attached to stanchions.

They also glide over us
in V formations northwards
to feeding grounds or their roost.
They could be ruling the edge
of the known world, levelling
the horizon, or adjusting
apparatus we never thought
was set wrong. Some fly close
to the surface then bank towards

swell, so that up-draught lifts
them over. They might be testing
gravity or the Earth's rotation.
Afloat, they look top-heavy,
may capsize any moment.
Getting airborne requires
faster wing beats, a clear run.
But once up, ungainliness
turns to grace. They're mended.

Notes

THE FISHERMEN: this villanelle was inspired by a photograph of me and my brothers, Norman and Peter. It shows us with the perch we caught early one morning at Llangorse Lake, Breconshire, in the early fifties. Lines were thrown without rods, conifer cones were used as floats and earthworms as bait.

THE RADAR GIRL: a fictional account of a radar girl's experience of tracking aircraft and flying bombs at RAF Bawdsey in the Second World War. I'm grateful to the following factual accounts for providing much valuable detail: *Radar Days* by Gwen Arnold; *Bawdsey – Birth of the Beam* by Gordon Kinsey; and *Shout and Whisper*, a Bawdsey Radar Trust Oral History Project 2010, compiled by David Heath.

FIRST DAY AT THE CENTRE: Archie and family were helped considerably by The Dame Vera Lynn Trust School for Children with Cerebral Palsy, based in Sproughton near Ipswich. Sadly it closed in 2015 due to lack of funding.

OPENING THE LOCK: this poem refers to three famous paintings by John Constable expressed through the eyes of the lock keeper at Flatford Mill. It was written as part of the 'Managing a Masterpiece' project in 2013, in response to the rich artistic history of the Stour Valley.

THE INNKEEPER'S WIFE: a poem in response to a collective imaginary examination of The Nativity by the Felixstowe Café Poets.

PENCIL WORK: this poem was inspired by reading *Birds of the Antarctic*, a collection of Dr Edward Wilson's drawings, paintings and diary extracts, edited by Brian Roberts. Born in 1872, he died with Captain Scott and Henry Bowers in 1912 on their return from the South Pole.

www.ingramcontent.com/pod-product-compliance
Lightning Source LLC
Chambersburg PA
CBHW032213040426
42449CB00005B/575